PARENTING HANDBOOK

TEACHING YOUR CHILD TO READ NATURALLY

PARENTING HANDBOOK

DONNA CASTLE RICHARDSON, ED.D.

TATE PUBLISHING
AND ENTERPRISES, LLC

Published by Tate Publishing & Enterprises, LLC
127 E. Trade Center Terrace | Mustang, Oklahoma 73064 USA
1.888.361.9473 | www.tatepublishing.com

Tate Publishing is committed to excellence in the publishing industry. The company reflects the philosophy established by the founders, based on Psalm 68:11,
"The Lord gave the word and great was the company of those who published it."

Book design copyright © 2016 by Tate Publishing, LLC. All rights reserved.
Cover design by Samson Lim
Interior design by Gram Telen

Published in the United States of America

ISBN: 978-1-68270-136-2
Family & Relationships / Babysitting, Day Care & Child Care
16.04.01

This book is dedicated to my children,
Scott and Heather.

Acknowledgments

The author gratefully acknowledges Jennifer Watson and Christy Richardson for recommendations on editing. A special "thank you" to Lisa Glover for the photos of her beautiful children.

Ed the cat recommends that parents interactively read with their children every day to make books come alive. Books can be a **cat**alyst for building stronger relationships by talking, reading, and listening.

A parent and child can begin reading together by cuddling up with a favorite children's book. Begin by having the child sit in your lap or close beside you so that you can encircle the child with your arms and hold the book in front of both of you. Parent and child must be able to view what is being read and discussed. This creates an atmosphere of a perfect mixture of love and reading. Creating a positive association toward books and reading begins at home during the magic of story time and the reading of bedtime stories.

When my little girl was three years old, I was reading a book to her as she sat on the sofa close beside me. She said to me, "Mommy that's not the way you read a book." She crawled into my lap and put the book in front of us. She then said, "This is the way you read a book."

Ed the cat suggests that parents use a technique called P-R-R-R-Ring through the book.

P-R-R-R-Ring through the book is the process of interactive reading where the parent and the child talk about the pictures in the book or story content throughout the reading of the book. During this experience, the adult shares what is being thought while reading to child, and the child is allowed to observe in a *safe and supportive environment* with a parent thinking aloud while reading. The parent is sharing what is being thought aloud during the moving in and out of the text when reading the book. Open and honest sharing between parent and child is important. The next pages should explain further what the P-R-R-R-Ring process is.

Predict, Read, Respond, Reflect, and Re-read

Begin using the first step in this interactive reading cycle of P-R-R-R-Ring through the book by looking at the pictures in the book, talking about the pictures, and discussing what the words actually say. Using the five senses is important for the first part of exploring the book. Looking at, talking about, listening to, and touching the surfaces of the cover and pages in the book provide positive early experiences with books. Touch, feel, look, and smell the wonderful aroma of a book. Today, tablets and videos bring another perspective to books that should be explored.

The time spent reading together is essential for the child to get a feel for books through observation, discovery, exploration, and experimentation. Take time to look at the book just before and/or after reading. Think of the child on an adventure of discovering a new world with each new book. The same experience can be used when reading a tablet, yet it is just a different way to look at books. Videos and audio cassettes of books can be used for follow-up.

The first step of P-R-R-R-Ring through the book is to...

Predict by "<u>thinking-talking aloud</u>" about the story

When reading the book for the first time, talk about the pictures on each new page to encourage the child to **predict** what is going to happen. Ask the child, "What do you think is happening in the story? Let's read the story to see how close you were in your thinking." Also, make connections by discussing what has already happened in the story. Talk about what you and the child have just read on the previous page to model "thinking-talking aloud" so the child will remember the story. The story content creates a foundation for thinking and remembering and is essential to developing comprehension skills now and later. Help the child make connections between the pictures, the written language, and personal life experiences, when possible. Connecting the book to the child's previous experiences helps the child see the relevance of the story and helps memory.

"*Thinking–talking aloud*" *is a process that the parent shares with the child by talking to the child about what is happening in the story. The child, also, responds and interacts by thinking-talking aloud by moving in and out of the text and pictures to confirm predictions, read aloud, respond to the content in the book, clarify, and remember the story or information. The adult and child share thoughts before and after reading a page in the book. Learning how the child is thinking provides insight into how the parent can support the child. This takes time, but provides the child with a model for early thinking about reading.*

Move to step two of P-R-R-R-Ring through the book to...

Read aloud to "<u>model how</u>" to read for the child

After you have talked about the picture on the page, show the child how to **read** by reading the page aloud. Repeat the pattern of predicting then reading throughout the book. Reading the book aloud provides a reading model for the child to see and imitate. Once the child has predicted what he thinks is going to happen, you can **read** the page to check out the child's prediction.

Preschool children will enjoy hearing the story read by an adult. For the school age child, parents should support the development of reading over time by being a reading model. Learning to read independently and fluently occurs over time. Parental support during the early years of reading is essential as the child develops confidence in reading independently. Predicting can also be done with chapter books related to content and thinking about what is being read and forecasting possible next events in the book. Guessing the end of a chapter and the end of a book is motivation to continue and find out what really happened.

Older siblings can read books to younger siblings using thinking-talking aloud. Parents should set aside a special time to read with the child by setting a time for reading during the day.

At bedtime, a child is generally quiet and wants to spend time with the parent. Bedtime can be a special bonding time when parent and child continue talking and thinking aloud about books.

Move to step three of P-R-R-R-Ring through the book to...

Respond to reading to "<u>clarify</u>" thinking about what is happening in the story.

Next, talk about what was just read. In other words, *model "talking-thinking aloud"* in **response** to what the book actually says. **This active talking and thinking aloud with the parent and child together will build a foundation for thinking and clarifying during reading when the child learns to read silently alone.** When responding to what was read and predicted, the parent is modeling *how to think about* what is being read. Talk about the child's prediction. Ask the child if the prediction was right. Talk about what was predicted accurately. Respect the child's thoughts and encourage thinking. The parent is showing "how" the mind works. This is a time to build connections from what the child knows to new perspectives and thinking. Making associations promotes the thinking process by helping the child see relationships between and among things and ideas.

If the child's prediction was the same as what happened in the book, celebrate together. If not, talk about how close the child's prediction was to the story and content. Talk about how the child's prediction made sense even though the author wrote something different. Encourage the child's **"talking-thinking**

aloud" by helping the child to self-correct if the prediction was different from the story. The parent's response to the child's prediction needs to be helpful and support the child to make connections between what the child predicted and what was actually written by the author. This is a time to discover how reading makes sense, even when the story is different from the prediction. Clarifying predictions build the child's confidence in reading.

Incorrect predictions should be discussed in a positive manner by building on what the child thought. For example, "Why did you think the next fish was a trout?" Let the child know it is okay to think differently from the author, but remember what the author actually wrote to reinforce comprehension and remembering. When the parent is talking-thinking aloud, the child observes and experiences a successful reader modeling, clarifying, and thinking aloud what readers do in their mind during the reading process. Talking with the child about the predictions and clarifying builds language and understanding.

If the child was close to the author's meaning in the book, use the prediction to talk about why the child thought something would happen. Teach new *vocabulary or language* by talking about what was said and meant in the book. Talking about what the child thought and what the author wrote builds connections about new information from the story. For example, if you are reading *The Teeny Tiny Tadpole* by Donna Castle Richardson and the child predicts "pond" instead of "lake," this is a wonderful teachable moment for vocabulary development. Talk about the difference between a pond and lake. Explain how a lake is bigger than a pond. Also, discuss additional vocabulary for other large bodies of water, such as the sea or ocean. Where a person lives will relate to the child's experiential reference. This type of discussion provides a time to expand vocabulary and clarify likenesses and differences.

Move to step four of P-R-R-R-Ring through the book to...

Reflect upon what was read to enhance memory and comprehension.

Encourage the child to go beyond talking about the book. This step of reflection helps the child remember. Reflection moves beyond clarifying and responding to the content of the book to build a foundation for emphasizing the importance of remembering. In this step, P-R-R-R-Ring focuses on building strategies for future comprehension skills. During reflection, the child begins to put the story together to remember all of the content. This is a time to focus on remembering what was read from start to finish. Talk about the story in the book. If the book has new information, talk about what the child learned. Talk about how the child views the book. This can be a time for remembering and evaluating the book. Questions such as "Why did you like the book?" can be asked. This step in P-R-R-R-Ring through the book provides time to focus on the content of the story as told by the author.

This is a time to put the story together in a sequence. Remember by *talking-thinking aloud* with the child, the parent is showing how to think while reading. This is a time to make connections in making the story meaningful. The child begins to see the importance of remembering what was read and observes the parent using comprehension strategies. These strategies can be used later to achieve reading success.

Move to step five of P-R-R-R-Ring through the book to...

Re-Read the book again

Ed the cat recommends a second reading to focus on fluency by using expression to read smoothly through the story for pure enjoyment. After the parent and child have P-R-R-R-Red through the book the first time, read the book again together from beginning to end with limited stopping.

> *On a special note: Some children may have shorter attention spans, and the child may be ready to move on to something different. Follow the child's lead. Bedtime is usually a quieter time when the child is relaxed.*

The adult can use a finger to point to each of the words while reading aloud. By pointing to the words during the beginning phases of learning to read, the parent can teach and show the importance of left-to-right and top-to-bottom page progression, which is an essential skill for beginning readers. After modeling how to read the story smoothly, model simply using the eyes to read, without pointing, to transition to mature reading behavior. Once the book has been read by P-R-R-R-Ring, the second reading can be a time of pure enjoyment for both parent and child. The parent can model reading fluently with expression through the book. Character parts can be added, when relevant. The second reading of the book is a time for expressing "feelings" while reading. During the second reading, the parent can model reading the book fluently and smoothly from beginning to end.

Parents or grandparents reading together with the child should be a wonderful time together for families to enjoy books. Set a time for the family to read a book together for pleasure. Young children will enjoy picture books while older children will enjoy chapter books. Reading builds the foundation for life-long learning.

Interactive Reading Cycle Strategies

Favorite books that encourage sharing the reading process together can be enhanced with interactive reading strategies. Another way to involve the child in rereading the book is to stop reading and let the child read by filling in a word, repeating a phrase, simply reading, or repeating a familiar sentence. If the book has repeating patterns, let the child read or say the repeating pattern throughout the book. *The Little Engine that Could* by Watty Piper is an example of a famous pattern book with a repeating phrase **"I think I can. I think I can."** *Selecting books for the child which includes repetition will encourage parent-child interaction as the phrase is repeated throughout the book.*

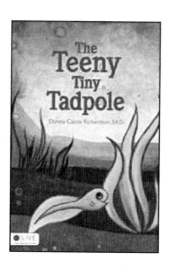

In The Teeny Tiny Tadpole by Donna Castle Richardson, the child can:

- Repeat the refrain, "The teeny tiny tadpole swam quickly away,"
- Say character parts of the fish or tadpole, and
- Add the cumulative body parts of the frog in the story during the transformation from tadpole to frog.

Encourage the child to:

Share the reading process

As the child becomes immersed in reading, create a supportive environment by reading together. Try different ideas such as stopping at the end of the line and letting the child finish. Basically, follow the lead of the child. The child will often create a way to participate in the story which the parent can follow and encourage.

Retell the process

Remember, after reading the story, encourage the child to retell the story from beginning to end. Return to the book when the child has difficulty remembering the sequence of events or important facts. *Support* the child to promote memory of the sequence of events or important facts in the book. Return to the book together to check out and clarify events and facts.

Return to the book

Ed the cat recommends that the child be given the book to explore. The parent or adult can move away, but be ready to support and respond to the child's questions. Go back to a page to clarify what was read if needed.

By reading new and rereading favorite books, the child will begin to make more connections to the actual reading process from the parent's reading model. However, older siblings and other adults can learn to do the interactive reading strategies just by observing the parent reading and using the strategies with the younger sibling. Over time, the child will become ready to solve problems. Natural questions for thinking about words will begin to be a part of the interactive reading process. Both the adult and child will begin to interact with questions. The study of words can be a part of returning to the book. Returning to the book to talk about words and letters can expand reading strategies. Examples of questions might be:

- "What does the word start with?"
- "Does it sound right?"
- "Does it make sense?"

Be sure as a parent or adult to act as the child's cheerleader when exploring and discovering how to read. Each child is different, some will

- want to explore and hold the book,
- go through the whole book, or
- want to leave the book to go on to something else.

The child's attention span will vary with books, time, and situations.

Most important is to follow the child's lead.

More Ideas for Reading Together

This book has been designed to provide parents and caregivers of young children with strategies that may come naturally or need further explanation. Other ideas have been added for encouraging other strategies to use during the interactive reading process and talking-thinking aloud introduced in the book. P-R-R-R-Ring provides a sequential process for thinking about and modeling reading with the young child. This reading together interaction takes time but provides a special time between parent and child.

In selecting books, it is important to begin with pattern books containing folktale characteristics such as refrains, repetition, and other types of repeating patterns. Additionally, books need to focus on the child's interests. Some children love concept books focusing on numbers or the ABCs.

To do interactive reading together parents or siblings can do **"talking-thinking aloud"** and sharing the reading process. A variety of strategies can be done such as

- point to the word or words while reading,

- encourage the child to finish a sentence by guessing or saying the last word (cloze),

- read the page or paragraph together at the same time (unison),

- read a sentence, then let the child read the sentence again (echo),

- encourage the child to repeat the repetitive parts in the book (refrains),

- encourage the child to say or read the character parts (part reading),

- pretend to be different characters in the story (acting),

- use different tones in the voice to read character parts,
- stop reading and talk about the book to encourage understanding of what was read through interactive questions and answers (talking-thinking aloud),
- talk about the characters,
- discuss the setting where the story takes place,
- continue to revisit the story text to clarify and remember details,
- encourage the child to retell the story sequence,
- discuss whether the child liked the book, and
- compare the book to other similar and favorite books.

Select books for the young child that have

- patterns such as repeating phrases,
- quotation marks for part reading,
- rhymes, and
- pictures connecting to the words on the page.

Select concept books for learning such as books that focus topics such as

- alphabet letters,
- numbers,
- colors,
- shapes,
- prepositions,
- opposites, and
- informational books.

Ideas for Word and Book Exploration

Explore and play word games with books. The study of letters is important. Returning to the book to study letters and sounds makes the learning more meaningful. The exploration of words in books can provide endless activities. Matching and seeing how words are alike and different can be a fun activity for the child.

Provide time to look at **alphabet** letters in the book by encouraging the child to

- find letters in the child's name,
- look for letters in other family member's names,
- point to the first letter in a word,
- name letters in the book,
- find words alike,
- look for repeating words, and
- talk about how words end by looking for rhyming words.

Provide materials for the child's exploration of **word study** after reading, such as

- magnet letters for matching letters and words in the book,

- magnet, plastic, or wooden letters for creating new words,

- alphabet cereal to create words,

- paper and pencil for copying words from the book,

- crayons or markers with paper to draw pictures and add descriptive words about the story,

- notebook with a pencil for writing an adaptation of the story,

- favorite words written on small cards that the child knows from the book,

- chalkboard or dry erase board for the child to write words or draw pictures,

- play dough to make letters, or
- rice in a shoebox lid or low plastic container for writing letters and words with fingers.

Play word games to develop **vocabulary** as you talk about the story, by highlighting

- specific words to prove predictions,
- rhyming words,
- repetitive words and phrases,
- events, characters, and ideas the child remembers from listening to the book being read,
- connections in the story to things in your family's life, and
- songs or chants in the book.

Books can be used to

- talk about words and pictures,
- point to words while reading from left-to-right and top-to-bottom,
- talk about the cover of the book,
- research the authors and artists, or
- find similar books.

Create games for **wordplay** to learn about different types of words through questions.

- What rhymes with *cat? Sat, hat, bat...*
- What does the word *car* make you think of? (associations)
- What is the opposite of the word *up? Down* (opposites)

- Think of other words that mean the same as *big? Huge, gigantic...*(synonyms)

- What is the first letter sound in each word of the title of the book, *The Teeny Tiny Tadpole*? (Alliteration) How is the sound *th* in the word *th*e different from the T sound in the other words in the title?

- What is a word that sounds like *pear*, the fruit, but has a different meaning such as pair of socks? (homonyms)

Use Books to Create Meaning

Write stories using wordless books to encourage the child to

- tell the story from the pictures in the book,

- copy words telling the story,

- dictate a story from the picture,

- copy words on a card to cut up later for a word puzzle, or

- select photos of your child and make a story about the child's similar experience.

Remember the story in the book by encouraging the child to tell the story from memory to

- tell the story from memory,

- draw a picture of favorite character,

- draw a picture of favorite part of the story,

- go to places in the book when possible,

- create a place in your home to act out the story, or

- video record the dramatization.

Show the child how to write. Talk about the letters while writing. After modeling writing, provide writing paper and markers for the child to explore. Set out a box of writing materials with markers, pencils, and crayons for the child to use. Find a variety of paper in colors, with lines, and in a variety of sizes and shapes for the child to experiment with copying and writing. Also, add child's scissors to the box. Set up a special place such as the table in the kitchen, den, or child's room for following up after reading a book. The kitchen is an ideal place while the parent is cooking, but still available to answer questions as needed. Be available to answer the child's questions during the creative process of drawing and writing.

Other important things to do

- follow the child's interest,
- talk about what is happening to provide language to experiences by writing what the child says,
- set up space for the child to draw and write,
- read books, magazines, and newspapers together,
- encourage pretend reading,
- set a time to read together daily with the child,
- show the child how to write words, or
- act out all or parts of the story.

**Select and use strategies
that work with the individual child.
Remember each child is unique and different.**

References

Baily, Alison L. and Margaret Heritage. (2008). *Formative Assessment for Literacy Grades K-6*. California: Corwin Press.

Baines, Lawrence. (2008). *A Teacher's Guide to Multisensory Learning—Improving Literacy by Engaging the Senses.* Alexandria, Virginia: Association for Supervision and Curriculum Development.

Burns, M. Susan, Peg Griffin, and Catherine E. Snow. Editors (1999). *Starting Out Right*. Washington, D.C.: National Academy Press.

Fountas, Irene and Gay Su Pinnell. (1996). *Guided Reading.* Portsmouth, New Hampshire: Heinemann.

Hattie, John. (2009). *Visible Learning*. London: Routledge Taylor and Francis Group.

Hattie, John. (2012). *Visible Learning for Teachers*. London: Routledge Taylor and Francis Group.

Hoyt, Linda. (2000). *Snapshots—Literacy Minilessons Up Close.* Portsmouth, New Hampshire: Heinemann.

Marzano, Robert. (2004). *Building Background Knowledge for Academic Achievement*. Alexandria, VA: Association Supervision and Curriculum Development.

Morrow, Lesley. (1997).*The Literacy Center.* York, Maine: Stenhouse Publishers.

Nelsen, Marjorie and Jan Nelsen-Parish. (1999). *Peak with Books.* 3rd Ed. Thousand Oaks, California: Corwin Press, Inc.

Orzkus, Lori. (November 6, 2014). Keynote Speaker: *"Comprehension and Guided Reading: Best Ever Literacy Survival Tips."* Edmond: Oklahoma Association Supervision and Curriculum Development.

Pinnell, Gay Su and Irene Fountas. (1998). *Word Matters.* Portsmouth, New Hampshire: Heinemann.

Portter, Jana, Judy Blankeship and Laura Carlsmith. (1999). *So That Every Child Can Read...America Reads Community Tutoring Partnerships.* Portland, Oregon: Northwest Regional Educational Laboratory.

Thompkins, Gail. (2003). *Literacy for the 21st Century.* 3rd ed. Upper Saddle River: Pearson Education, Inc.

Thompkins, Gail. (1999). *Update to Literacy for the 21st Century—A Balanced Approach.* Upper Saddle River: Pearson Education, Inc.

Vaughn, Sharon and Sylvia Linan-Thompson. (2004). *Research-Based Methods of Reading Instruction Grades K-3.* Alexandria, VA: Association for Supervision and Curriculum Development.

Yopp, Hallie and Ruth Helen Yopp. (1996). *Literature-Based Reading Activities.* 2nd ed. Boston, Massachusetts: Allyn and Bacon

CPSIA information can be obtained
at www.ICGtesting.com
Printed in the USA
LVOW01s0909300816

502372LV00010B/34/P